Say What You See

Eat

Rebecca Rissman

Raintree is an imprint of Capstone Global Library Limited, a company incorporated in England and Wales having its registered office at 7 Pilgrim Street, London, EC4V 6LB – Registered company number: 6695582

To contact Raintree
please phone 0845 6044371, fax + 44 (0) 1865 312263, or email myorders@raintreepublishers.co.uk. Customers from outside the UK please telephone +44 1865 312262.

Text © Capstone Global Library Limited 2013
First published in hardback in 2013
The moral rights of the proprietor have been asserted.

Edited by Rebecca Rissman, Daniel Nunn, and
  Catherine Veitch
Designed by Philippa Jenkins
Picture research by Ruth Blair
Production by Victoria Fitzgerald
Originated by Capstone Global Library
Printed in China

ISBN 978 1 406 25141 8
16 15 14 13 12
10 9 8 7 6 5 4 3 2 1

British Library Cataloguing in Publication Data
Rissman, Rebecca.
Eat. -- (Say What You See!)
394.1'2-dc23
A full catalogue record for this book is available from the British Library.

Acknowledgements
We would like to thank the following for permission to reproduce photographs: Shutterstock pp. title page (© ravl), 4 (© Nattika), 5 (© karamysh, © Petr Malyshev, © Bratwustle), 6 (© Ieva Vincer), 7 (© Petro Feketa, © Analia Valeria Urani), 8 (© discpicture), 9 (© trevorb), 10 (© Gunnar Pippel, © Monkey Business Images), 12 (© 3445128471), 13 (© .shock, © corepics), 15 (© Africa Studio, © Jiri Hera), 16 (© JohanKalen), 17 (© Andrey Armyagov, © Firma V), 18 (© ssuaphotos), 19 (© T-3, © .shock, © oknoart), 20 (© Rob Marmion), 21 (© MikLav, © Gorilla), 22 (© Monkey Business Images); Superstock pp. 9 (© Flirt), 11 (© Blend Images), 13 (© Fancy Collection), 14 (© Corbis), 15 (© BlueMoon Stock).

Cover photograph of a girl taking a bite out of a watermelon reproduced with permission of iStockphoto (© Kim Gunkel).

Every effort has been made to contact copyright holders of material reproduced in this book. Any omissions will be rectified in subsequent printings if notice is given to the publisher.

Contents

Breakfast is cooking... Say what you see!

stirring

Pouring

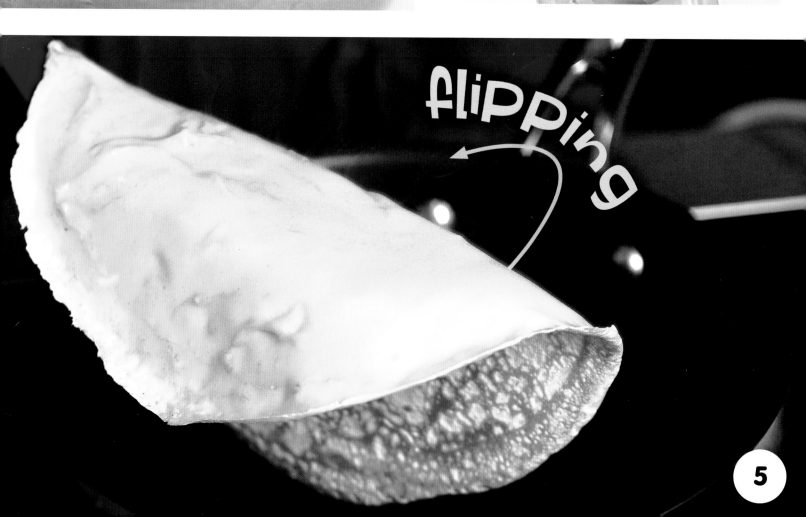

flipping

peeling

Baking

whisking

Boiling

Scrambling

It's nearly time for lunch...
Say what you see!

Crunching

Slurping

Slurping

Slicing

Grilling

Blending

Tossing

Scooping

Dipping

Spreading

Chopping

It's dinner time...
Say what you see!

Twisting

Chewing

Cutting

Roasting

Rising

Melting

Steaming

Eating gives us energy for...
growing!

Playing!

Thinking!

21

We eat to be healthy...
and because food tastes great!

Can you find these things in the book? Look back... and say what you see!

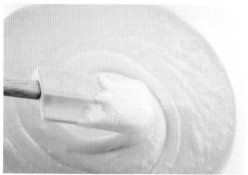
stirring

slicing

crunching

melting

Index